GW00993549

LESTER SUMRALL

MAN WAS MADE FOR TRANQUILITY

TROUBLE OR TRANQUILITY?
THE CHOICE IS YOURS

MAN WAS MADE FOR TRANQUILITY
ISBN 0-937580-62-7
Copyright © 1990
Published by LeSEA Publishing Company
P.O. Box 12
South Bend, IN 46624

CONTENTS

1
Tumultuous Living
Can Kill You!

"The Lord is my shepherd;
I shall not want"
(Psalm 23:1).

Some of the most tranquil and healing words in human literature are found in Psalm 23. It is also probably the most familiar passage in the Bible. The Jews, both Orthodox and Reformed, know this psalm. So do Christians of all denominations. Moreover, you will find the world even knows this psalm—you will find them, for instance, asking for it to be used at funerals. The question comes to mind: Why? Why is Psalm 23 so well known and so loved by those who really know and appreciate what it is saying? And why is it requested by those who don't fully know and appreciate its rich meaning?

A PERSONIFICATION OF PASTORAL TRANQUILITY

Among other things one could answer by saying man is well adapted to a nature-oriented life; that man's constitution is such that he was made for a peaceful existence. Psalm 23 presents a classic portrayal revealing what man was created for and how he should live. It is a picture of pastoral tranquility.

ENTER DISOBEDIENCE

Was it God's intent when He created man that they would live anything but a peaceful existence? Tumultuous living can kill you. We all know what happened as a result of Adam and Eve's disobedience. The beautiful tranquil environment, the innocence of man, and the perfection God intended, as well as man's fellowship with God, was spoiled. When the serpent cast a shadow of doubt on the word of God, man as a responsible creature became irresponsible, succumbing to the wiles of the devil.

Because God's created beings turned aside from God, it became necessary for God to deal with and judge them.

THE APPEAL OF TRANQUILITY

A little background on Psalm 23 is helpful in fixing in our minds why it is so loved and so important in the world's literature. The Psalm speaks of green pastures, still waters, paths of righteousness and fear of no evil. That was strong appeal in a world of tumultuous living.

7

David, you may recall, was the shepherd boy called from tending sheep to become king of Israel. He was God's man, certainly not his father's choice.[1] The youngest son of Jesse, David tended his father's sheep.

Psalm 23, therefore, along with Psalms 22 and 24, are called shepherd psalms. They depict our Lord as the Good Shepherd, the Great Shepherd, and the Chief Shepherd. We see Christ in these psalms. There are those who wonder if the psalm was written when David was still a shepherd boy or when he was an aged king. The more popular view is that this is the song of an old shepherd. David the king never forgot David the shepherd boy. I think he always had the heart of a shepherd. These are the musings of someone who has gone through much trouble. David was writing from the depths of human experience; his life had known both song and shadow, victory and privation and hardship. And therein lies its appeal.

"THE LORD IS MY SHEPHERD"

While the world may claim to love this psalm and the essence of tranquility it represents, actually it is not for everybody. You cannot claim Christ as your Great Shepherd, unless you have acknowledged Him as the Good Shepherd who gave His life for His sheep.

Think about the tranquility there is in a peaceful countryside scene with only one person present— the shepherd—and his sheep. Visualize the sheep moving slowly, grazing as they go, with a little brook nearby to quench their thirst. As the rays of the sun warm the earth, the sheep lie down underneath the shade trees beside the brook in peace and safety. That is the picture David gives to us, drawing from his memory bank, as he recalls those days when he led his sheep along good paths, rescuing them with his rod and staff when they strayed. The rod was for defense, the staff was for direction. They were meant for comfort.

The psalm speaks of the Lord's table, of communion with Him (vs. 5); it speaks of the Holy Spirit (vs. 5) and the anointing that comes from God. When David said "My cup runneth over," he was referring to the joy in his heart that undergirded him. And when he said, "Surely goodness and mercy shall follow me all the days of my life: and I will dwell in the house of the Lord for ever" (vs.6), he was acknowledging that God had brought him all the way from the green pastures and the still waters to where he was, and to where he was going (heaven and a prepared place).

INWARD DISORIENTATION

The Bible tells us of another beautiful and tranquil place, the Garden of Eden, the home of our first parents.

Thrust out of the Garden, Adam and Eve experienced the inward disorientation that has characterized mankind ever since. God's good plan was spoiled. The beautiful setting of the Garden of Eden was now to be but a memory for them. The Fall resulted in innocence lost, attempts to cover up their sin, and violent change and disruption in their lives—disorientation and disruption that were to be passed on to all their progenitors, including the world in which we live today.

But Christians are the fortunate ones. They have more orientation than any other people on the face of this earth. When they live according to God's Word, they are assured of direction.

AN UNCHANGING GOD

God has not changed. When the Bible reveals God, among other attributes we learn of One who does not change. Malachi 3:6 says, "I am the Lord, I change not" (KJV).

The New Testament amplifies on God's unchangeableness with these words: "Every good gift and every perfect gift is from above, and comes down from the Father of lights, with whom there is no variation or shadow of turning" (James 1:17).

The world today beats upon humanity like an angry sea. We read and hear of revolutions and wars, unrest, human suffering as a result of man's inhumanity to man, a collapse of all moral restraints, and conditions that are anything but tranquil.

People today are confused, they don't know where to go, what to do, whom to believe. That's why your testimony to the stability that can exist in one's life is so important—stability and peace that comes as a result of your confidence in God's unchangeableness, Christ's love, and the Holy Spirit's power.

---

1. You can find the complete story in I Samuel 16.

2

Trouble: Man's Common Denominator

"For affliction does not come from the dust,
Nor does trouble spring from the ground;
Yet man is born to trouble,
As the sparks fly upward
(Job 5:6-7).

Do you know anyone who is exempt from trouble? If you do, he or she must be dead. Man is born into trouble. Job's friend Eliphaz, actually the most sympathetic of his three friends, speaks true words in Job 5 when he tells Job that the problems of mankind, and Job's troubles, didn't just come from the dust of the ground.

A few chapters later in the book by his name, Job

comes on the scene and says almost the same thing as his friend: "Man who is born of woman is of few days and full of trouble" (Job 14:1).

Job is saying that trouble is a common denominator of mankind. All of us have trouble of some kind or another. Trouble is a universal language. We inherited it because of the Adamic fall.

It's what we do with that trouble, however, that separates the men from the boys. Trouble can make or break a man or woman. The choice is ours. It's up to you; it's up to me.

You can become depressed, discouraged and disgusted; or you can say with God's help you will be an overcomer. You can curse God, or you can recognize that as a believer you are on a collision course with the world, but you can claim God's promises and strength to endure in His name and be victorious over the trouble.

Like the Apostle Paul, you can say, "[Even though I am] hard pressed. . .perplexed. . .persecuted . . .struck down. . ." I am not "crushed. . .not in despair. . .not forsaken. . .not destroyed" (see 2 Cor. 4:8-9).

In living the Christian life we are not promised immunity from the harsh realities of living. The life of the Christian is not a sheltered exemption from trouble.

STRENGTH AND OVERCOMING GRACE AND POWER

God never promised a rose garden after Adam and Eve were expelled from the Garden. Instead, He spoke of thorns and thistles.

But what He did promise, He does provide, and that is His own enabling strength, overcoming grace and power. "In the world you will have tribulation; but be of good cheer, I have overcome the world" (John 16:33). Just preceding those words, He told them that in Him they could have peace.

Recognize it now, to be forewarned is to be forearmed. When you determine to follow Christ faithfully and without reservation, you will find there is a fundamental discord between yourself and what's going on in the world. Why should it be any different for you and me than it was for Jesus? The same spirit in wicked men that crucified Christ will persecute and oppose those who are His in the world today. Never forget it, the world put him on the cross and thought they had done away with Him. But the same power that raised Him from the dead, comes to you and to me today and says, "My victory is yours!"

He gave Himself for us once; now He gives Himself to us. And through Him we can say, "Who shall separate us from the love of Christ? Shall tribulation, or distress, or persecution, or famine, or nakedness, or peril, or sword?. . .Yet in all these things we are more than conquerors through Him who loved us.

"For I am persuaded that neither death nor life, nor angels nor principalities nor powers, nor things present nor things to come, nor height nor depth, nor any other created thing, shall be able to separate us from the love of God which is in Christ Jesus our Lord" (Rom. 8:35, 37-39).

3

The World and the Devil

"I am no longer in the world, but these are in the world. . .
(John 17:11a).

Yes, we are in the world, and so is the devil. The world is the devil's territory. It is estimated that by the year 2000 there will very likely be 10 billion people on earth.

What kind of a world are we headed into? What kind of people will populate this planet? What can you and I do about the world's people?

Civilization changes so quickly. We live in a day when a book can become obsolete before it is even printed, where some inventions have been superceded before they are patented. Changing people, changing times, changing conditions. A world whose face often reflects agony. A world brought into our homes via television so that we know within moments what is going on elsewhere on the globe. We are witnesses to history in an unprecedented way.

ON THE RUN

One of the gravest situations of our time is what I call changes in relationships. Hardly anyone today has what we at one time called "old friends." Old friends today can mean people we knew three months ago. We live so fast. We move so often. We are a world on the run.

We are fast becoming a rootless world. It would be interesting to find out how many people reading this are living where they were born and raised.

Good friends and a closely knit family are very stable forces in a society. With friends nearby with whom you have established a beautiful relationship you have someone to turn to in your lonely moments. But so many today live in virtual isolation, not even knowing their next door neighbors.

Children are growing up today without the benefit of godly grandparents who can have a wonderful influence in their lives.

Our cities are teeming with people who are rootless. Though surrounded by thousands, yet they are as alone as if they were on a desert island. To walk the streets of many cities these days is not a happy experience. I have done that, for instance, in New York City. In certain parts of the city the homeless and the destitute make your soul weep. I have wept in India, the Philippines, in Africa, as I have surveyed the scene in place after place.

Radical changes in our life situations can cause anxiety, stress and serious illness.

Change can cause confusion and trigger feelings of instability. We are living in a drug-crazed culture. That vacuum existing in every human's heart is meant to be filled by God and God alone. Man on the run reaches for something to fill up his loneliness and his hunger cravings. It should not be surprising that we find people turning to drugs.

Mysticism, spiritism, cults, and New Age religions are flourishing. This hunger and desire for fulfillment with no knowledge of the truth causes people to succumb to the supernatural.

The Chicago Tribune (Sept. 9, 1989) reported a growing teen problem in their psychiatric facilities throughout the city—youths dabbling in Satanism. The paper reported that psychiatrists are being "educated by [their] patients about the Satanic belief system," and "are getting their first chance to formally learn about Satanism and begin devising treatment for the increasing numbers of teenagers who are falling into its dark world of suicide, rage and drugs." What is happening in Chicago is happening worldwide.

Why are young people turning to Satanism? One specialist in Satanic beliefs who is seeking to ferret out the facts and develop a treatment program commented: "Often the most die-hard believers in Satanism are bright youths who never learned problem-solving and coping skills, saw their parents as religious hypocrites and achieved the only successes of their lives through the cults."

He went on to explain that they have big self-image problems and feel less competent, less powerful [than their peers and others] and Satanism offers power and a sense of belonging. "The cults, with their promises of complete individual freedom, regardless of consequences, and ultimate power, give them on a silver platter everything they've ever wanted: membership in a group, power, sex, drugs, freedom from guilt."

Satan is a deceiver and has been at it a long time beginning in the Garden of Eden. But where are Christians? Where are the churches who should be showing these young people that when their roots go down deep into Christ's marvelous love, they will experience an inward filling that satisfies. Where are parents?

THE BREAKUP OF THE HOME

You say, "Dr. Sumrall, what is wrong?"

The Bible provides the answer: "The wicked are like the troubled sea, when it cannot rest, whose waters cast up mire and dirt. 'There is no peace,' says my God, 'for the wicked' " (Isa. 57:20-21).

Certainly one of the factors contributing to so much of the turmoil in society today relates to the breakup of the home. I know of a woman whose home went to pieces and she went into a state of shock and has been mentally ill ever since. Her husband will answer to God one day for his selfishness.

Ask a woman why she left her husband and she may say, "I didn't love him any more."

17

My friend, that is why the devil was thrown out of heaven! He wanted things the way he liked them.

In contrast, Jesus in human form, prayed, "Father, not My will, but Thine be done."

When Jesus comes into your heart, you will no longer live just to please yourself.

Not only do adults suffer as a result of brokenness in relationships, but young people and children throughout the world are suffering dreadful anguish because parents would not work at living together in peace.

One of the ways we prove our love and obedience to God is in our marriage relationships. It is one demonstrable way of saying you are putting the Kingdom of God first in your life; that you want God's will more than your own way. You serve Christ best when you invest time and energy in your marriage relationship and your children.

Pornography the Destroyer

Every two minutes, a child is molested in America. I am convinced there is a direct correlation between child sexual abuse and pornography. According to the FBI, 90 percent of hardcore, illegal pornography is produced by organized crime. It is its third highest profit industry, after narcotics and gambling. An $8 billion a year business.

The head of the Center for Disease Control in Atlanta, Dr. James Mason, says, "Almost all of our sexually transmitted diseases are out of control. . .I can't help but believe that pornography is a significant contributor."

The Bible teaches to avoid even the very appearance of evil and to have nothing to do with the unfruitful works of darkness, but rather to expose them (see Eph. 5:11).

Pornography disturbs the spirit, it is addictive, illegal, and a destroyer of normal human relationships. It is a demonic contradiction of normal human relationships. It is a demonic contradiction to God's plan, promoting physical satisfaction without caring love, sex without responsibility, and union without obligation for the consequences.

It was God's original plan for peaceful living that His created beings were to be fruitful and increase in number; Satan has sought from the beginning to center on this fundamental work of God. Pornography is one of the ways he has succeeded in doing this. Pornography is a child destroyer, a woman exploiter. Pornography is one of Satan's tools to wreck havoc upon mankind.

"A GENERATION AT RISK"

The present generation is being called "A generation at risk." A look at newspaper headlines and leading stories in the media reflect its pain and confusion:

The three leading causes of death among adolescents are drug-and-alcohol-related accidents, suicide and homicide.

Every year 1 million teenagers run away from home.

Every year 1 million teenagers get pregnant.

The remorseless brutality that characterizes the senseless killings and worldwide outbreaks of violence is so heinous, and the details so lurid as to make them almost beyond the understanding of sane human beings.

Here is just a random sampling of headlines from the newspaper and magazines:

Gunmen shoot down 17 Filipinos in church.

Somalia military kills 46 in unrest.

"Night of terror" kills 13 as shells bombard Beirut.

Outmanned and outgunned, police are feeling the stress of the drug war.

Neighborhood can't forget Rice murder.

Jones teen ordered to stand trial in death of father.

5 children die, 30 hurt during school rampage.

War on streets being waged in nation's capital.

Murdered leaders—The list goes on.

Number of juvenile offenders climbing.

JESUS' BURDEN:
THE INTERCESSION OF CHRIST FOR US

Before leaving this world, Jesus prayed a long prayer to the Father found in John 17. It is often referred to as His "high-priestly" prayer. He prayed these things for believers: (1) their protection (v. 11); (2) their sanctification (v. 17); (3) the unity of believers

(vv. 21-23); and (4) the ultimate glorification of believers (v. 24). Essentially, it was His intercession for those who would comprise the church (vv. 6-26).

If you want a good verse for the mission of the church, it can be found in this passage: "As You sent Me into the world, I also have sent them into the world" (v. 18).

God in the flesh, looking down the aeons of history, foresaw the devil seeking to rise up and make havoc of the life of the church. He saw the church in the world, "And the world has hated them because they are not of the world, just as I am not of the world. I do not pray that You should take them out of the world, but that You should keep them from the evil one" (vv. 14-15).

The life of the Christian in this world is of living in the midst of conflict and tremendous spiritual battle. I think, for instance, of Ephesians 6 where the Apostle Paul exhorts us to "put on the whole armour of God" in order that we may be able to stand in the evilness of the times in which we live.

It is a world of tension. Not tranquility. The picture Paul portrays in Ephesians 6 is of a world in battle. Not peace. Because we belong to Christ we are the targets of the enemies of Christ, and they are many. They are the "principalities, powers, rulers of the darkness of this world, and spiritual wickedness in high places."

The devil's one overriding ambition has always been to mar and destroy God's perfect work. In Christ we have a wonderful position and condition. We have been covered by Jesus' prayer. It was a prayer for our protection. A prayer for God to keep us. Are you sure you are under that covering?

4

The Anchored Christian

The Lord knows the way of the righteous
(Psalm 1:6a).

Christians need deep roots. Spiritual drifting should not characterize the life of the stable Christian, that is, the one who is rooted and grounded in the love of Christ (see Eph. 3:17).

Strength in the inner man comes as Christ dwells in our hearts by faith (see Eph. 3:16-17a). Steadfastness in our daily Christian walk comes as we are rooted and built up in Christ (see Col. 2:7).

That will not come, however, if you are a church drifter, running from one church or meeting to another, tanking up supposedly, relying on spoon feedings instead of seeking out the truths of the Word and spending time with God, knowing what you believe, and believing what you know.

This is what provides real stability and peace in the inner man. You won't have a nervous breakdown with the tranquility God gives inside of you.

CANDOR IN PRAYER

God has graciously provided a way for us to communicate with Him. Think about it. That's awesome. That we can actually make contact with the Almighty.

He wants us to be unreservedly honest with Him through prayer. Candor in prayer is our blessed privilege. You can't be forthright with someone you scarcely know. But you can be like an open book with someone you know intimately and trust implicitly. That's the kind of relationship we are to have with God the Father.

Prayer is a stablizing force. A power that spans space in a split second through words on our lips. In a world of turmoil, prayer can give tranquility. All around you may be in chaos, but you know that peace that passeth understanding because you are in touch with the Source. However, our prayers are only as powerful as our lives.

God does not hear the prayers of the unrighteous. The ungodly do not have an audience with the Father in Whom there is no variableness (see James 1:17). Remember, He is a righteous God, a God who changes not. And His face has always been turned against wickedness. He cannot countenance that which is unrighteous. The psalmist declared that God saves the upright in heart. "God is a just judge. And God is angry with the wicked every day" (Psalm 7:10-11).

Moses declared that all who behave unrighteously are an abomination to God (Deut. 25:16). Their prayers get no higher than the ceiling.

There is only one way to have an audience with God. It comes through repentance: "Seek the Lord while He may be found, call upon Him while he is near. Let the wicked forsake his way, and the unrighteous man his thoughts; Let him return to the LORD, and he will have mercy on him; And to our God, for He will abundantly pardon" (Isa. 55:6-7).

James said, "The effective, fervent prayer of a righteous man avails much" (James 5:16b).

CENTERING IN ON THE WORD OF GOD

There is power in the Word. To know the Word and be able to wield it against the powers of darkness is to be able to rout the devil and his hosts. That's what Ephesians 6 is all about—protection for believers through the whole armor of God. The weapon we use is the sword of the Spirit, which is the Word of God (Eph. 6:17).

Studying God's Word can anchor you down. We have come to that time in history when we are going to have to learn how to live; if we don't, the devil will have a heyday.

This world is not a playground although millions act as if it is in their hedonistic pursuit of pleasure; but it is a battleground. Too many who claim to be Christians, however, want it both ways—enjoying Christ and the world too. You can't go along with worldliness and say you are living according to the Word.

Do you, like the psalmist, say words to this effect to your Maker: "Your testimonies are wonderful; Therefore my soul keeps them. The entrance of Your words gives light; It gives understanding to the simple. . .Direct my steps by Your word, and let no iniquity have dominion over me. Redeem me from the oppression of man, that I may keep Your precepts. Make Your face shine upon Your servant, and teach me your statutes. Rivers of water run down from my eyes, because men do not keep Your law" (Psalm 119:129-130, 133-136).

Do you weep because the world does not live according to the Word?

The stresses and strains of life are reduced as the Word of God enters our hearts controlling our thoughts, impulses, words and actions.

THE TRANQUIL HOME

Tranquility in the home comes as we love our families and seek to obey what the Bible teaches about relationships within our own four walls. The instructions to husbands, wives and children can be found throughout the Word of God. The one word that encompasses all of the Christian graces which are to characterize these relationships is love.

If we treated our own family members as nicely as we do some of our friends, our families would love us more. Wives are told to be submissive "as is fitting in the Lord." Husbands are told to love their wives and to not be bitter toward them. Children are instructed to obey their parents in all things because this pleases the Lord. And fathers are told not to provoke their children, lest they become discouraged (Eph. 3:18-21).

Husbands are told that answers to their prayers will be hindered if they are not treating their wives in an understanding way, and if they are not honoring them "as weaker vessels, and as being heirs together of the grace of life" (1 Pet. 3:7).

Wives are told what their conduct is to be, how they are to dress, and what kind of a spirit they are to have (gentle and quiet) (1 Pet. 3:1-6).

Every beautiful attribute that belongs in the daily life of the Christian is not to be shed when family members enter the door of their homes! The fruit of the Spirit—love, joy, peace, longsuffering, kindness, goodness, faithfulness, gentleness, and self-control— each of these should be demonstrated toward one another as family members.

PEACE THAT SURPASSES UNDERSTANDING

Peace in the life of the Christian comes as we practice the presence of God. First there comes peace with self as the Apostle Paul talked about in Philippians 4:5-9:

"Let your gentleness be known to all men. The Lord is at hand. Be anxious for nothing, but in everything by prayer and supplication, with thanksgiving, let your requests be made known to God; and the peace of God, which surpasses all understanding, will guard your hearts and minds through Christ Jesus.

"Finally, brethren, whatever things are true, whatever things are noble, whatever things are just, whatever things are pure, whatever things are lovely, whatever things are of good report, if there is any virtue and if there is anything praiseworthy—meditate on these things. The things which you learned and received and heard and saw in me, these do, and the God of peace will be with you."

Then Paul says, when we live like that, we can experience peace in our circumstances. There can be contentment regardless what state we are in (v. 11). "I know how to be abased, and I know how to abound," he said. "Everywhere and in all things I have learned both to be full and to be hungry, both to abound and to suffer need. I can do all things through Christ who strengthens me" (vv. 12-13).

God can be trusted to supply all our needs, Paul said, "according to His riches in glory by Christ Jesus" (v. 19).

HOW TO GET ANCHORED

We need to get anchored. We are in danger of being blown, pushed, and tossed about. I heard a doctor say that possibly 90 percent of all sickness is caused by emotional distress. That is what we have been talking about in this book. If we can get our insides at rest, and our inner being at peace with God, we will know the joys of a good and God-blessed life.

Our relationships with family members need to be carefully nurtured; and so do our relationships with those with whom we work, as well as our friendships. Be faithful and loyal to all those with whom you live, work and play.

The Book of Psalms opens with a wisdom psalm that stands as a faithful doorkeeper to the entire Psalter. It reminds us of the righteous behavior and fruitful life that are characteristic of the one who delights in God's law (vv. 1-3), in contrast with the life and destiny of the ungodly (vv. 4-6), who will perish. The Word of God is our hallmark of faith and practice. When that is so, we are spiritually healthy and fruitful; in contrast, the wicked are spiritually dead and stand guilty before God.

The writer of Psalm 1 had discovered the secret of tranquility: "Blessed is the man who walks not in the counsel of the ungodly, nor stands in the path of sinners, nor sits in the seat of the scornful; But his delight is in the law of the LORD, and in His law he meditates day and night" (vv. 1-2). That is the anchored man, the pure-hearted man. That is the well-adjusted person.

"He shall be like a tree planted by the rivers of water, that brings forth its fruit in its season, whose leaf also shall not wither; and whatever he does shall prosper" (v. 3). We are not rootless saplings; we are mature and strong with deep roots. Our lives bless others. People in the community can say, "Thank God for that person, they are an example to the community." We are not to be takers but givers and producers, and the more we give of ourselves, the stronger and more prosperous we become.

"The ungodly are not so, but are like the chaff which the wind drives away. Therefore the ungodly shall not stand in the judgment, nor sinners in the congregation of the righteous" (. 5).

That is where our nation is today. We are like chaff being blown from coast to coast, from one country to another. We are fast becoming an immoral people living on the edge of chaos. Chuck Colsen says we are standing on the brink of a dark new age. The very pillars upon which our civilization was founded are being eaten away, eroded, undermined.

"[But] the Lord knows the way of the righteous, but the way of the ungodly shall perish" (v. 6).

That is the way of the anchored ones. God wants us to be strong in that which He provides. He wants us to live as godly, good people in this sin-darkened world. His promise is that He will keep us tranquil, at peace kind of people, when our minds are stayed on Him (see Isa. 26:3).

YOU, TOO, CAN BE SAVED!

I ask you: If you're not born again, if you are not *sure* where you'd go if you were to die RIGHT NOW, please ask Jesus into your heart. He will give you peace, and joy, and hope!

You need a personal Savior, a personal commitment to Him who is able and willing to forgive you of ALL your sins. Pray this Sinner's Prayer, and really MEAN it.

"Lord Jesus, I am a sinner. I believe that you died and rose from the tomb to save me from my sins. Forgive me by Your grace for all the sins that I have committed. Wash me with Your blood, and I shall be clean. I ask You into my heart right <u>now</u>. Be my Savior and my guide forever. Amen."

In your flesh, you may not FEEL any different. But, the Word of God tells us that you are now a New Creature, and old things are passed away and forgiven. You are no longer under condemnation. You are in Christ Jesus and you now walk after the Spirit.(Romans 8:1, II Corinthians 5:17, I John 2:12, Luke 7:47)

Now that you have become a child of God, please write and I will send you a little pamphlet titled "So You're Born Again!"

Write to: **Lester Sumrall**
Box 12, South Bend, Indiana 46624.

GLOBAL
FEED-THE-HUNGRY PROGRAM

While Lester Sumrall was in Israel in 1987, the Lord spoke to his heart about initiating a global program to combat hunger. That was the beginning of the the End-Time Joseph Program to Feed the Hungry. God declared that the agressive attack against the forces of evil should be three-pronged. How can this be done?

1. **We will feed the hungry.**
2. **We will strengthen churches with pastors' seminars.**
3. **We will hold evangelistic crusades with proclamation of the gospel.**

We are looking for 10,000 pastors to challenge world hunger by including "Feed the Hungry" in their missionary giving. Laymen are asked to join "The King's Court" and laywomen are asked to join "The Queen's Court" to fight world hunger. By becoming a part of the End-Time Joseph Program to Feed the Hungry, you will be kept informed as to what you can do. For more information, write:

FEED THE HUNGRY, South Bend, IN
46680-7777 USA

Let us hear from you today. We must act now! Tomorrow may be too late!